Home
and
Away

Also by Rachel Wetzsteon

The Other Stars

Home and and Away

POEMS

RACHEL WETZSTEON

Penguin Poets

PENGUIN BOOKS
Published by the Penguin Group
Penguin Putnam Inc., 375 Hudson Street,
New York, New York 10014, U.S.A.
Penguin Books Ltd, 27 Wrights Lane, London W8 5TZ, England
Penguin Books Australia Ltd, Ringwood, Victoria, Australia
Penguin Books Canada Ltd, 10 Alcorn Avenue,
Toronto, Ontario, Canada M4V 3B2
Penguin Books (N.Z.) Ltd, 182–190 Wairau Road,
Auckland 10, New Zealand
Penguin India, 210 Chiranjiv Tower, 43 Nehru Place,
New Delhi 11009, India

Penguin Books Ltd, Registered Offices:
Harmondsworth, Middlesex, England

First published in Penguin Books 1998

1   3   5   7   9   10   8   6   4   2

Page vii constitutes an extension of this copyright page.

LIBRARY OF CONGRESS CATALOGING IN PUBLICATION DATA
Wezsteon, Rachel.
Home and away / Rachel Wetzsteon.
p.   cm. — (Penguin poets)
ISBN 0 14 05.8892 2
I. Title.
PS3573.E945H66   1998
811'.54—dc21   98-4489

Printed in the United States of America
Set in Granjon
Designed by Betty Lew

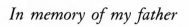

In memory of my father

ACKNOWLEDGMENTS

I'm grateful to the editors of the following journals, in which some of the poems in this book were first published:

Boston Review, "A Rival"
Boulevard, "Narcissus on the Move"
The New Republic, "Poem for a New Year"
The Paris Review, "Home and Away," xli.–l.
Partisan Review, "Surgical Moves"
Southwest Review, "Pomona," "The Triumph of Marsyas"
Threepenny Review, "Clubfoot," "Learning from the Movies"
The Western Humanities Review, "Chasing Spring," "In Memory of W. H. Auden"

An excerpt from *Home and Away* (xli.–l.) appeared in *Best American Poetry 1998*. I'd also like to thank the Ingram Merrill Foundation, Yaddo, and the Sewanee and Bread Loaf Writers' Conferences for their generous support.

CONTENTS

IV

I
Home and Away

i.

Long before us, the kindling dried, becoming
liable to burn; the buzzards circled, hoping
tempers would rise and clinches become bloody
after the stately branches of the past gave
way to rough paws in bushes. And before long
new fires will rage, the buzzards double back from
excellent meals on hearing that the strollers
suddenly think of knives and target practice
even as they wear out the walkways, dancing.
But the great hand that holds us between fingers
cannot hold one poor candle to this new fist
squeezing my heart; the vision on the bench there
suddenly makes me brush my coat of ashes,
though flames leap up on either side of the park.

ii.

Smother me in your color and your clangor,
eager forest; let me in on your fun!
There is a bench where it is always summer
and as I hurry toward it, winking nature,
in on the secret, meets my overflowing
heart with a healthy dose of outer weather,
long lines of green trees play out the occasion.
But, idiot pursuer, to be stood up
is an insulting joke not to be stood for;
solid oaks flaunt their barks in mocking contrast
to my unsettled insides, with their
horrible freaks of nature: hot snow, huge lack.
Taunt me with your excesses, leafy monsters,
knock me down with the fullness of your boughs.

iii.

Skulking around a park bench gives you time to
think about all the fools you might turn into
when you sit down. I will not build a strobe-lit,
brutally run panopticon for lovers
so that I know which tricks are worth avoiding;
I will not lose my pride and hide in bushes,
hoping to learn which base acts last the longest.
What I am forming is a list of people
never to be: the squadrons of the half-dead
stalking the park in search of volunteers to
give up their blood; chameleons of the soul
eyeing the better benches from the near ones;
losers who think themselves the greatest winners
ever to tell a lie or make a heart break.

iv.

These are the enemies we must contend with,
shadows on our internal walls to see and
flee from, human hurdles to jump over.
But we cannot avoid them so completely
that we can claim to be the world's first wooers;
every new road to heaven rests on old ones,
and if we level with ourselves about it
our bird is not the phoenix but the grackle,
struggling to stay aloft. For all these reasons
I serenade the bench by making faces,
come to you armed with guns and gallows humor,
knowing the park is full of foes, but vowing
never to let them win until they put our
lights out. That would be raining on the flame.

v.

If I did the proper thing and sat down,
would the motive get up, leaving us with
memories of sitting down, dim hopes of
someday sitting elsewhere? In one version
parking myself next to you and staying
means the park sprouts roads that open onto
wildly churning fountains, promising a
fertile open space in all directions.
But there is another version, one where
mean trees, closing in on us like gunmen
tracking down a target, send down roots that
harden into rocks, encourage leaves to
block the distant view out, only making
far-off sounds of running water louder.

vi.

Standing there like someone struck by lightning,
picking every impulse into pieces,
next time you go through all this fuss, remember
life on the bench is not a simple constant
to which you can retreat when life gets hairy,
stupid or scary: chaos rules here also,
making the bench so frighteningly cluttered
that I no longer know which sweet face made you
notice me in the first place. Often, when I
sense your displeasure, I am ugly Vulcan
fumbling with tools; a kind look means I'm fair and
fearless as Achilles; and when you first
showed up, I was Philomel when our eyes met,
Helen when you sat yourself down, and smiled.

vii.

Suddenly a passerby on horseback
gives your fickle torso such a swivel
that I must stick needles in my own to
reassure myself of my existence,
a technique which works until I see the
rider's similarity to you—these
gallopers have long since left the park grounds
when we make up stories of our conquests,
wondering, behind dark glasses, was it
all in the head, in the underfed, well-read head?
When a renegade or a redeemer
goes by so fast with its enchanting features,
what can the unhinged onlooker do
but stay up all night, staring at the footprints?

viii.

What is it about my destination
that turns each trifle on the way into
a landmark, makes each tiny obstacle
a giant of a challenge? You would think
the god of love would outfit me with blinders
so I could reach the bench a little faster,
but goal of mine, your halo is contagious;
the vendor catches it, the public fountains
spurt champagne and warble in your honor,
and blades of grass regale me with so swift
and intimate a wave that I prefer
the bent paths to the straight; on no account
would I give up the bench for the adventure,
but getting there is always half the fun.

ix.

Eating apples in the park at noon,
I knew that nothing much would come of it;
there was no joyful, terrifying feeling
that I was just the latest in a line
of guilty nibblers. And you, hasty ones
who strutted in as though you were important,
you may have done your time with golden legends
but nothing rubbed off: you were not my type.
But when I look you in the face and see
the multitude of mothers you come after
and all the distant fathers you prefigure,
when you are both yourself and something greater,
what pleasures crowd a moment! For this reason
the park is roomy, and the park is dark.

x.

Why are you stopping? Was that a shot in the park?
Will they come after? Keep your head down and go,
foresight or no. Prove to me that you are not
one of them. Would these eyes lie? As you sat there,
what were you thinking? Thinking of what to say
in case you sounded stupid or went away.
Anything is possible. Don't even
talk that way! And you? That you could never
fit in the robe I'd sewn for you. And did I?
Call it a passing tremor. Is that your hand
circling my neck? It is. Why are you frowning?
Call it a hunch. Is something missing? Do you
welcome a warm hand, will you come with me to
foreign lands, other forests? I do, I will.

xi.

When I was still a moper on the bench
and shut the local shapes and colors out
by looking at the backs of my own eyes,
it was the place I always pictured there:
all down the bridges and among the domes
a giddy couple wandered, lighting lamps,
and if a loving pair was what it took
to turn a cityscape from brown to bright,
both pair and city gained from the exchange—
it gave us history, we gave it life.
Or so I figured, moody on the bench,
my prospects low, my hopes insanely high.
A vision came and carried me away
and put my roaring guesses to the test.

xii.

There are some places where you go to hide,
and others where the reds are reddest if
your heart is in ten pieces; somehow when
I landed here, I knew it was a place
where two extremes existed at one time.
But how can we, two little smiling guests,
compete with all this pain? It would be good
to shed tears here for some elusive thing
that broke your heart and left the bits behind;
it is a perfect place to breathe a sigh
because a nagging thing has been removed;
but smiles will never get you very far
in this rare city poised somewhere between
seeking and losing, fantasy and crime.

xiii.

Every year they marry the sea and sky,
but you can see it happen every night
when darkness brings the elements together:
apogee holds nadir like a lover.
Everyone considers it a custom
fit to copy; couples come from miles to
modify the myth into the wedded
bliss; but one long sober look at sunset
makes the cynic or the romantic in me
swear to shun the leveling effect that
turns clouds wet and wild waves into silent,
pointy tufts of color, makes me wonder
what has become of boundaries that matter—
the far sky, the unsinkable horizon?

xiv.

They say a carnival does not know footlights.
That was before a carnival became
a place to bring your megaphones and notes to
rather than a basement with a shelf
where you deposited your worldly goods
and stored your inhibitions. When we dance
a wan voice says repeatedly that dancing
breeds forgetting; when we drink, a blinking
neon sign asks whether we have joined
the boozy crowd yet; when we take our masks off,
new ones take their places; when we sleep
we dream of waking up; and when I wake
I put the party down in spiteful writing,
beating out a rhythm on your back.

9

xv.

When looking at the sun is all the rage
and bands of tourists hobble by on stilts,
hoping for a passing glimpse of God, but
seeing a sky the color of gunmetal,
let us reinvent the art of squatting,
spending all our waking hours learning
how the river leaves its watermark,
why the crack has kept the house from crumbling,
where the danger threatened, and then vanished.
What if our inquisitiveness brings us
face to face with some unpleasant answers?
What if our trip takes us to a brick wall
where a hand has written "Get me out of . . ."
dying before finishing the sentence?

xvi.

Boatman, turn your rudder on the stained glass
and take me to the islands of the blown;
when I am done, a glittering flotilla
will waft me and my painted treasures home.
But why does this green demon overtake me
now, of all times, here, when I should be
corrupted by the proper gem I came with
and not the false ones of the marketplace?
I would attribute it to native greed
if I did not remember times when buying
was what a body did to keep a mind
healthy enough to want; that past, it reaches
wild heights, craving brass gondolas, a plastic
model of the square, complete with doves.

xvii.

Blasphemy, the bells toll, blasphemy,
though similar events were what sustained
the city through more threats than it could count:
keep the new blood coming, and you keep
a sinking isle afloat. But they soon learned
that filling up a place is not the same
as rivalling its beauty; boys grew sad
because the act detracted from the room
where it occurred; young wives leaned out of windows
to see the city stretching out before them—
the roofs all red, the river spun from silver—
and said a hurried prayer before retiring:
forgive me for competing with your glories,
forgive me for believing that I could.

xviii.

City of disease and faded pigments,
special case most golden and serene,
it is not your island bliss we love
but what came after; out go peace and calm
and up go our stalled heartbeats, skyward climbs
our limitless affection. If a city
beckons to its former self with one
brisk wave, it might as well be Switzerland—
healthy and sweet-smelling and still ticking
but not the place for us. Not in its prime
but in its fertile, glorious decline
is when a city makes our pulses soar,
our spirits hunger. Like impatient rats
we bide our time while azure fades to black.   *11*

xix.

But lying in a black room, wide awake
and sorting through the highlights of the day—
a house that stones and lions could not save,
a wall whose color crumbled in our hands—
I'm suddenly suspicious—no, confused—
about the train of thought that brought us here:
if sickness and decay are what it takes
to get a new life off to a good start,
do we haunt empty squares and rank canals
in order to confirm our own fresh scent?
Or is it (this is where the tossing and
the turning start) that we crave glimpses of
that red and rotten city where we're bound,
however far we travel when we leave?

xx.

I stared out of the tiny window, stared
until all I was looking at was air,
and all the things I loathed when I was there
gathered around me and began to tell
my fickle sinking heart how much I'd miss
the domes at every corner, and how much
I'd struggle to resist the brutal split
of cities into "here" and "all the rest."
A show of kindness drew me from the view.
This was the future I was headed for.
We made a stab at speech: "Good trip?" "No . . . yes . . ."
"Why are your eyes all watery and red?
We've had our outing, now we can go home."
"Love still has something of the sea," I said.

xxi.

From the center of the giant room
almost all the paintings looked alike,
but then one caught my eye: a soothing square
of burgundy, surrounded by black dots
and bordered by a plain gold frame. At last
I worked my courage up and walked its way:
a battle scene explained the burgundy,
the black dots were burnt branches—someone's idea
of pathos?—and the frame now gleamed with shells
and overripe fruit. I looked away in shock,
only to find that all the other paintings
were thrown into new, startling relief:
the cool remoteness of a dead madonna,
the heart-stopping mystery of a Dutch interior.

xxii.

Man jumping, says the caption. Man enthroned,
we say, by all the poses that are his:
the pinnacle is flanked by all the squats,
kicks, efforts and absurdities that make
a pinnacle a feat. Eternity
is what grows thick around a runner's leap,
just as a city shines more brightly when
all time is simultaneously there.
But as we look, his strength becomes our shame;
we'd rather have the leap without the squat,
the swift descent without the memory
of what it felt like to be hanging where
no hand could touch us, no old photograph
show us two jumpers, rooted to the ground.

xxiii.

The realists and the red-cheeked people say
you're not supposed to linger in this room,
or else the presences who hover here,
wearing their intimate and static smiles,
will dazzle you until you choose a face
to follow, shun your friends and will not leave.
These things are not supposed to happen; when
I pair your image with the one up there
my reason says that motion, mayhem win.
But what fast lane could be as moving as
the hand that holds the grapes that never rot,
the romance of a slowly turning head
that never meets your moist eyes all the way
but goes on doing what it does so well?

xxiv.

To turn from a great painting and behold
another face as water-logged as yours
is to approach a pleasurable brink
without the penalty of falling off,
and just as you have honored, or abused
the painting by surrounding it with stories,
now you invest the fleeting newcomer
with attributes you cannot live without.
Someday these strangers, leaving loved ones safe
at home, will reconvene in a big room
where speaking is forbidden (it would soon
distort the vision) but a night of silence
shows the seated gallery of mutes
the raucous, airborne art of the possible.

xxv.

They do not know each other, but it's clear
they're dying to be introduced by some
matchmaker of a barmaid—who, perhaps,
has seated them together with this goal
in mind. And in their wretchedness, they're two
of a despondent kind: his battered hat
and puffy downcast eyes, her bitter smirk
and apathetic slouch are signs that they
have nothing to look forward to except
more trips to the café to stare at stains,
a daily tally of near-misses, and
a nightly intake of a drug to dull
the senses—call it absinthe, call it sleep.
All this would change if they could only meet.

xxvi.

They know each other. What else could account
for their frenetic undisguised attempts
to stare at walls, at shoes, at anything
that will not stare back? Even the eavesdropping
barmaid, getting restless, leaves the two
to stew in their own juices, which they do:
what started off as strange resemblances—
those eerie moments in the birth of love
when someone seems to read your mind—became
excess of knowledge, looking at a face
and finding nothing new there. His grim hat
pulled over grimmer eyes, her whimsical
distracted glances, hide their thoughts of those
they would have met if they had never met.

xxvii.

The clever mirror dawdles down the lane
and faithfully reflects the things it sees:
a steeple glints, an alleyway becomes
a dead end. Into this big room we come
with bright ideas about how we're the ones
adroitly rising, terminating there.
And as one mirror fades, another one
takes over. We're blind fools, we're liars, but
strange faces, other places, please forgive
our wild imaginations; when you leave
a hall of haunting colors having failed
to leave your mark behind, you must confront
a life of unrecorded ups and downs,
a timeless moment, dying at the door.

xxviii.

What makes you think she's up to something bad?
Look at her eyes; you do not get that sly
by thinking saintly thoughts. If I were asked
I'd say he was the one to be afraid of.
In that hat, can you blame him? More than that:
his shifty eyes and pale face are clear signs
that she should pack and leave. Then why are their hands
so confidently interlocked? Hands, bands—
one must keep up appearances. The dog
who wags his tongue at us—why is he smiling?
Appearances do not fool dogs; they smell
a crime before it happens. And the mirror
hanging on the back wall? Regard it well:
two witnesses are in it, two reflections.

xxix.

This marble head will never bat an eye,
let alone create a scene. So why,
when we observe her high up on her plinth,
do we so badly want to take up stealing?
We could stick the poor thing on a coat rack,
cover her in clothes and show her sunlight;
we could stay inside and squint and squint
until a notion could be seen to gleam
in her expanding eyes; we would be wrong
if we supposed the rays and flashes came
from those two sockets. She can only stare
at all our plots—I would say haughtily,
but severed heads on slabs can only stare.
She wounds because her eyes are blinder than love's.

xxx.

There is a column and there is an arch
half sunk in earth. This scene does not exist
and no one is pretending that it does;
the caption reads, unhelpfully but not
without a certain truth, "capriccio."
We go to it, for we have spent some time
roaming these imaginary landscapes;
the views were wonderful, and if you fled
from bed at night, I always knew where to find you.
But when the tourists started showing up—
finding fault with everything—we bolted,
heading for museums, where fat guards clucked
multiple tongues: there goes, they said, that couple
making up stories for the thousandth time.

xxxi.

Our moods do not believe in each other.
Mourning monks imagine quiet lives
paced out on marble; lovers in a clinch
forget the storm that sent them scurrying
to separate places. Violently we're tossed:
a stabwound tends to take attention off
a letter framed, another letter makes
the stabwound seem so trivial it might
as well be all healed. But with all the moods
that fight for space, occasionally some
reminder of a former one remains:
during vespers, someone swears he sees
a pillar burn; a barbecue disbands
when someone finds a snowflake on her sleeve.

xxxii.

Down the desperate red lane they go,
and all the barroom brags are proven true:
when soothing fluids coat your aching valves,
both love and war take place at one remove.
It is like watching rainfall from a hill
or climbing fatal crags in padded boots;
while other lovers fondle knives, you hear
your double wailing in another room,
and when the one whose depths you tried so hard
to plumb comes toward you, you indulge in all
the seedy nighttime pleasures that the stern,
right-minded day denied, but find that when
you wake, it was not you they happened to—
the awful price of numbness and of lust.

xxxiii.

Remember when the white cat crossed our path
and we made it go faster with our laughter?
We were so delighted with ourselves
that we believed we'd altered a cliché,
until we saw that what had made it run
was not our laughter, but its own right ear
or what was left of it: a bloody stump
that dripped and bubbled, and a stubborn fly
that nestled in the ooze and would not move
had made the poor thing quick. There is a band
of thugs that go around attacking cats
and some of them resemble you; I will
tuck in my tail and run as I recall
the fears, the joys of trying to be white.

xxxiv.

It used to be that what is called the good life
caused a lofty raising of my brows
when I went out; I never could respect,
let alone be, a member of that club
whose loves cannot take place in plain rooms, and
whose lives are sad redundancies: they wear
seductive clothes to take them all off faster,
they hold their glasses high, and drink to supper.
What never struck me on my moral throne
was that these couples swallow down their pride
with grains of bitter salt; to enter bars
in fancy get-ups, marking up the menu,
is to postpone the moment, hours later,
when brilliant shapes descend, unveiled and empty.

xxxv.

So much goes on inside a snowing globe
that movers, suns and shakers never see:
examining the cold thing on its shelf
they thank their stars that they don't live that life
of wait, whirl, wait; it's passion in a void,
they think, then gallop westward in their spurs.
But as they ride, the snow is riding too:
those whorls of white that eddy, then abate
before they even gather steam, mean more
when they are framed by frost on either side;
those endless waits that turn the bowl into
a catacomb become endurable
when dormant flakes recall an old storm for
the dangerous, doomed fury that it was.

xxxvi.

I'll pivot on the barstool and pretend
the world's a giant runway; all those years
of studious eye contact never could
fulfill the baser itch in me, but now
I'll be an eye, examining spare parts,
I'll look and look and be glad I can't love.
Fair shape, I will consider you: you're like
a hilly, grassy landscape famous for
a quarter of an hour, then so dull
you send explorers fleeing; you're a house
with pearly knobs and knockers and a voice
that purrs "Come in," then leads me to a room
beyond which you have never tried to go.
I crumble like a lover at its door.

xxxvii.

Wise owl, you are not wanted in the snow.
Your methods and your mastery come later
when our protective sheets of ice have melted
and fearful children stagger into sunlight,
full of blinding spite and troubled insight.
Perceptive owl, vacate the simple forest
and take your caliper and spyglass with you,
or leave them here as tools that we may find
and set up shrines for, happy in our stupor.
Sophisticated owl, you never leave
without a warning hoot, a fluttering
of branches: on a typical adventure
we set off smiling, only to discover
the forest floor is littered with your feathers.

xxxviii.

The pretty girls are retching on the stairs;
the men are getting warm inside their suits;
the house grows lighter as the sun goes down
and cats are howling, let the chase begin.
For longer than a vision takes to fade
I was a willing member of this world
and walked inside the avalanche of limbs,
the piles of open mouths and rolling eyes
with my own secret plans to pick and choose.
But soon the mouths became a scarlet mist,
the limbs were obstacles to upper rooms;
I stumbled to a garden far away
and waited there, through summer and through fall,
for what the kinder winter months would bring.

xxxix.

Love, when the meter cannot read the weather
the sun gods hurry home, and we come out,
putting on white coats to keep the few,
large men on horseback who patrol the forest
from seeing us—or thinking us sane creatures—
as we make our way down rows of graves.
If your nimble fingers or warm shoulders
do not brush me, do not think I mind;
never touching means never killing
the sultry ghosts who always walk three steps
in front of us. What was summer like?
Frozen in time, we have no need to know.
What cloudy times await? We cannot see them
under a fading canopy of snow.

xl.

After all the lights in the sky die down,
brutally smothered, we will still be dancing;
watch the smile I flash and abandon as I
hook you around the waist, then fling you out.
Such commotion has its appeal—whenever
you become too warm, I abjure you, and when
I'm cold I pull you closer. But to keep you
locked in a clinch or spinning into orbit,
stunningly as it makes our outfits flare and
sparkle, has its drawbacks. As we go on,
I cannot help the urge to fling you further,
pull you back more roughly. Witnessing
our special brand of dancing from a distance,
someone might mistake it for a fight.

xli.

How different any house looks from outside
and from within. I used to circle mansions
finding out, through guessing and good luck,
what acts of kindness kept the home fires warm
and what was done in dens. Now all unpacked
I feel the leaping flame below the floor,
my dreams consist of madly smoking chimneys
turning into smoking guns. All you
who covet life behind closed doors, look out
for changing views: safe homes can be deceiving
and dusty corners, formerly the mark
of depths unsounded, or of time well spent,
become the cold, grey, fuzzy, wooly monsters
that fill the head before an idea forms.

xlii.

I walked among the gorgeous unturned stones
with rising hopes, a pickaxe and a plan:
the answers I scraped free would be the bricks
I'd use to build a green and spacious home,
and in this place of knowledge I would glue
wild eyes to lush walls, grateful for the gleams
my mystery, my spur had sent my way.
What I could not predict was that there comes
a time when there are no more stones to scrape
the mossy truth from, that a house composed
of all the answers that I schemed so hard
to get could get so grey. My cellmate and
my stone, who could have known that there was such
a thing as knowing someone else too well?

xliii.

Acting in accordance with your wishes,
let us try a quick experiment:
buy a house and set it down on firm soil
and, completing all the steps required,
fill it to the brim with embryo yous.
When little creatures hang from chandeliers
and steal your treasured hours, ask yourself
the reason for the choice: was it to fill
the wanting world with more endangered lives
like yours? Was it to cauterize old wounds?
Was it to see yourself forever blended
with a beloved other? If the first,
sheer hubris; if the second, lots of luck;
if the third, when water blends with oil.

xliv.

The oldest story in the book has just
revealed another chapter. There are no
competitors with bedroom eyes who send
encoded notes; no juvenile excuses;
no trio of bored, beautiful delinquents
who flutter past on bicycles, intent
on cigarettes and scandal. In their place
there is a pyramid without a base
on either side of which, the rival lives
of rugged climber, deity of parks
and doomed, descending homeowner, are stationed.
Sometimes they meet in a productive summit
but even then, they cannot miss the sight
of skating eros, red-faced at the bottom.

xlv.

Something, love, is singing in the shower
but it is not me; all the spouts are on
but rather than warm water, I suspect
a flood of doubts comes crashing on my brain.
Wise fools have always said that when you woo,
a breathing world surrounds you; what they save
for later revelations on the stairwell
is how you stand there, listening for clues
leading to the arrest of household objects.
Accessories I use to tame my hair
remind me of the hairpin turns we used
to skirt; cigar butts, fuming in an ashtray,
form just a tiny portion of the troops
gathering daily in this screaming house.

xlvi.

Provocateurs and spies have been among us,
sensitive eyes who knew what we were up to
when we exhaled tornadoes; and when they were
dead to the world or elsewhere, there were portents:
great gusts of rain approved our resolutions,
sunshine meant watch and wait. But in this big house
nobody seems to notice; I could drop hints,
swallow a capsule or a morning toad,
or I could claw the walls until the day came
and there would still be no one there to see it,
no way of telling my heart was not in it
except the banner of decisive action,
the calling of the sharp, impatient helper
that rattles in the cupboard, set on escape.

xlvii.

Before I stab, a moment of polemic:
little fish, aspiring to be big ones,
cannot observe a couple without smirking,
avidly drain the color from our lives
until there is no unrest in our room
except the paper flame that they would put there
to fuel their furnace: we become an excuse.
Great unveilers, chroniclers of the warzone,
certainly talk of the eternal struggle
over the reins, but for our sake remember
there is no background as explosive as its
passionate foreground; get it through your head that
we are not cloth dolls with holes and bulges
but flesh in houses, killing with our own hands.

xlviii.

We may have our problems, rash explainer,
but at least we are not walking automata,
holding hands to keep a toiler busy,
getting mad to help a tirade along.
The forces of production knock on our door;
I scare them away by the timbre of my voice.
Ghosts barge in and reshuffle the blood on the wall
until it resembles a toolbit or a mother,
but the blood keeps pumping out; I stab and stab
because of a cruel word said the other day,
a grey hair found in the soapscum, a desire
to stop a head from cracking, and most of all
because of the face that flashes past your lashes
and is not mine. I stab at that flinty tempter.

xlix.

By this I knew I'd never leave my room
to look at cities, parks or art again:
the carnage was a comfort, not a care,
the thing that lay beside me on the bed
improved my mood because it matched the red
around the house, the red that ruled the world.
But even killers singing odes to gore
have lucid intervals. I thought of all
the faces that I never saw because
I was so busy welding them to views:
the bright eyes raised in ecstasy, the head
hung low in grief—for them I carry a torch
that lights the corners of my chamber as
I wait for sirens, as I wait for sleep.

l.

Sometimes the flames remind me of your good points;
other times, when I become too bold
and start believing that you might come visit
they leap as if to say, thus I refute you.
Who knows whether the things I do without you—
making shadow puppets on the walls,
giving private screenings of my crimes—
will cure me of the urge to do it over?
I only know that sometimes when the flames
are cool enough to walk through, I will risk
the shame of being found out by my keeper,
and the worse shame of never being noticed,
by standing at the red-rimmed, steamy window
through which, sometimes, a park bench will appear.   *27*

II

Abstract Aubade

i.

The sun, like some stupidly drunk party guest
turning over tables to prove his own drunken wonderfulness
while other guests nurse drinks, roll eyes, avoid him,
clambers over the last dispersing clouds
and happily shines, annoying joy-ball,
as if to shine were enough! What he lacks
is range; he could fall on fertile or fallow soil,
minister to the athlete or the cripple,
and the scene would be the same
and for this reason impossible to love—
a woman looking out a window
at her approaching suitor, will not warm
to his confident, hot rays if she knows
they could enter an empty room and be no different.

ii.

You, on the other hand, were helpless without me.
During our long night together
what a brilliant pair we made: I supplied
the bed and the board, and you provided
the boxes of nails, taught me the tricks
of howling. But nothing is the same now.
Tentatively, you lift your frown with
your fingers, and suggest I do the same;
you guiltily pace by the doorway;
you look from the window to me as if to say

is it so bad? And how can I contradict you?
Even I know there is much to be said
for soaking up sun in golden valleys, but
consider the marriage we might have made; extend
to a lifetime the lurid colors of our sorrow,
the tragedies by which we made the night longer.

iii.

You jiggle the lock, so I will be brief.
Seeing you so radiant at the window,
suddenly bronzed and healthy, made me realize
your departure was a sure bet anyway. Before,
when we huddled close in the smothering darkness,
I could not say, this is me, this is pain;
now I cannot forget it. But traitor, roam where you will,
I know you. Soon you will run back, all hunched over,
to that foggy park on the outskirts of town
where rabbits sob and decadent willows blow
and cry until I call you back; but so that
we better spend our next night together,
so that I can open the curtains and, letting
light do its bald-faced wooing, come to think of you as
a dead grief, a starless night's aberration, go now.

A Rival

Names flow from her mouth as so many hearty allies;
she's breezy host to a horde of stars
she keeps and scatters to her liking, Mr. A
of the flawless phrasing, Madame B, who has won
many prizes, astonishing Miss C (recently up
to no good), and sweet Sir X, of whom I may have heard.

Pert, able and a born joiner, she has done well
by a ruthless study of the golden room where
everyone matters, peering through curtains to catch
the unsurpassable swirl of a skirt,
straining to hear the guests' after-dinner laughter
and dancing their measures again and again until
she knew the password and strode grandly in
while outside, bard of the usual, I haggled with the bouncer.

Now, dazzling comes so easily that she seems
always to have been there. Robust with nurture
she inhabits the room in gowns of dreamiest satin
and often, as parties reach their pitch,
can be seen enchanting kings.
Annoying exile, *I* scud into snows whose
elegant steeps and hollows I find no voice for,
sit under frail skeletons of trees
whose leafless tops show the sky at its darkest
and whose roots, drowned in soil, can't touch me.

If life's a pose, no one can fairly blame her;
if, seeing me at the window late one night,
cold from the crazy paths of alien towns,
she shuts it and so forgets me (the distant tyranny
of shadows, the hot gnashing teeth of doubt),
it is ample recompense when in fragrant flavorful air,
warmed by a fire that has blazed for centuries,
she dips her pen in a lake of ink, and the pen flies.

The Late Show

And so it came about that there was no way
of crossing the river except by carrying
the special mirror, the one you found in your pocket
one winter. Orioles, crows flew over the water
and made your palms hot with lust and envy,
but to reach the other side and sit in those
ghostly deckchairs, tipsy on spiked
lemonade and insight, you need to see yourself
testing the waters. Menacing waves crashed
around a bend and broke over you;
the mirror showed a face half in love
with its own drowning. The bodies of dead dwarves came
barreling past; bales of hay were burning on the banks,
making fumes so thick that the stepping-stones
that really seemed to be getting you somewhere
showed up in the mirror as evil empires
crushing a mind that wandered where it wanted.
Saying "This way" was a way of killing those tics,
those changes of heart that made traveling fun.
When friends asked you what your trips were like,
you started pulling out the mirror and letting it
do all the talking. There on the table amid
childish inner tubes and cheap souvenirs,
it sang the praises of never getting there.

This method of fording streams having been
accepted, run with, a glossy gizmo
that loosely resembled your sturdier mirror

hit all the newsstands; travel accounts
turned cryptic and unwieldy, becoming
half-journalese, half-mandarin rambles.
A struggle became a reflex. And God only knew,
you were good at it: the stagy brow-mopping,
the true hopes of getting across, followed
by sloughs of sincerest despond, made the mirror
glint like no others. And the way fish appeared
in your glass was really magical, too:
we never knew whether you'd start describing
Jaws or a Triton. But after anyone
spends too much time with a mirror,
even its best views can start to seem
planted, not discovered. It should have
cut more, fit less easily into your hands;
sometimes when, observing your journey,
we saw a bit of river flash in your eyes,
we wanted more. We missed the time
when people like you schemed hard to start
shores bending and waves ascending. But most of all
we wondered whether you should have submitted
a little less easily to your fate:
no teleology drove you to it,
though there was, it's true, that vogue of coming
later rather than sooner. Great wader with a
hand-held mirror, what would you have done if the current
had carried it away for a day? Would the things
you saw in the rising tide have made
a duller but more intimate story?

In Memory of W. H. Auden

When there are so many intervening years
between a splash and its outermost ripples,
   when so many outpourings followed
  hot on the heels of your disappearance,

why heap another faded flower on your
already overloaded grave? That you changed
   the landscape of the mind forever,
  surpassed all others in range and insight

is no great surprise by now. But to one who
came a little late to the shore of mourners,
   looking over their shoulders turned out
  to provide a healthy perspective on

what went on there. Many who craved your mantle
had a way of only putting on pieces
   with the result that, scanning the shore
  for intimations of a successor,

one could not help noticing the mighty gulf
between them and you: at your wake they sported
   the tight coat of impressive learning,
  the formal outfit, frayed on the inside,

so that as they shouted your name to the sky
something was missing; where was one who could tell
   the sad, run-down city what ailed it,
  hold head and heart in such a tight balance?

If I rudely grabbed, in turn, for your halo
I would be not only mad but misguided;
   trying to be like you would be like
   setting brazenly out in a forest

with the intention of following, step by
step, a famous explorer's excavations.
   After you knocked the trees down for us
   we cannot very well do it over,

although the thought is tempting. There is one year—
my first, your fifth-to-last—in which our paths could
   have crossed. I sometimes picture the scene:
   stroller collides with old man in sneakers

and Saint Mark's Place falls silent for a second.
But fantasies lie. All I can hope to add
   to your magnitude is a sense of
   how it struck one who, twenty years later,

opened a book and opened a world that was
nothing at all like anyone else's; how
   little room you made for complaining,
   how you forgave your watch and your body,

and how you surprised us with obvious but
unexpected pairings—you knew that knowledge
   does not shun the lover's embraces,
   you knew that passion without precision

is like some awful parody of a book
on how to succeed: be one thing and be it
   exclusively, the book says, and fly.
   But if you fly like this, you will plummet.

You once described someone else's writing as
a crazy house of cacophonous voices—
   in the attic stuttered the spinster,
   in the gameroom the drunkard sat cursing,

and in him all was mayhem. But view this quirk
another way, and it looks like a virtue:
   your moods, more facets than masks, reveal
   the depth and breadth of the ideal person.

None of which should give the impression that you
went around adoring everything; it was
   the land surveyor's roving eye, not
   the blind affirmer's lecherous glances

that made your palette rich. But why, when the life
after death of even giants is shaky,
   when hard hearts are set on debunking
   and reputations are frail as spring buds,

do you forge on, a little wrinkled maybe,
but always upright, stepping blithely over
   the fatal trap set by attackers,
   the hidden snare of complete approval?

Probably because you are so various.
In you no words flaunt your inability
   to say what you really want to; we
   look in vain for a culpable symptom

of the system in which you are complicit,
skewer it though you do; you house no would-be
   parricides, chatting up their targets.
   Your stride is too slow and steady for that.

Thanks to your efforts you are safe, in short, from
ambitious projects which, more often than not,
 turn out to be—how well you put it—
 ephemeral pamphlets, boring meetings.

They do not know what to do with you, and so
they do nothing at all. For this be grateful;
 many have risen and fallen, not
 because of any inherent merit,

but because of a fickle set of pincers
which quickly plucks, and just as quickly drops them
 when the task at hand is done, or when
 a new one promises better results,

leaves more inroads temptingly open. A walk
with anyone else has a hushed agenda;
 smoothest routes to their destinations,
 windows in which to see their reflections

are what they look for when they go out. But you
took in the sights like a curious tourist:
 the dull stare of immigrant faces,
 the twilight glow of a watertower

caught your attention equally. And even
when your keen eye became (or so some argue)
 somewhat dimmer—no ones like to learn
 that someone who once looked at a country

and trembled, now finds it ever so comfy—
the spark remained, and the wandering pupils.
 And they remain still. You have taught us
not how to follow in your footsteps, but

how to carve out paths for ourselves, and if I
had my way with the elements, I'd have you
    know you are gone, but not forgotten:
    tender, impudent, cynical, joyful,

silent as a tidal wave, safe from the sands
of time, twenty years later you still show us
    not a room, but a way to light it,
    not a goal, but a way of arriving.

Another View of the Ideal Person

A rattle of avid hands, but the only thing really moving
is the heavy mahogany chair where,
checking a fact, tonguing a mint, she sits
facing the crowd and wanting it to be over.
The applause is thunderous, the aftermath
will be louder still, and she would be lying
if she lowered her eyes and said she didn't like it.
But good as the smiles are, they won't hold for her long;
nights like this are like getting rid of phlegm in public;
you cough it up and go back to what you're best at
and the crowds, if they choose to, build shrines or form
battalions. And so she shakes hands, without cunning, without all
those over-the-shoulder looks before
gut reactions turn into measured opinions.
Meanwhile, some factions, sharing their views, are
seduced by geldings; others are overheard saying
"Do drop by, I'm serving rack of guest."
Past the small sea of kind twos, cliquish threes
she fixes her gaze—some vision's gotten hold of her
and won't let her go. So tonight, it's the hall, the party,
the tense theater where they gather, some for the words,
some for the conversation; but long before morning
she'll slip out, as she always does, and wander
away from the spires to confront the snow,
planning another way of making it melt.

Poem for a New Year

Love that a reign of terror struck dumb,
love that, respectful, close and clinging,
never could match the thrill of distance,
   come away from the stunted creatures;
show me your stumps and teach me why they
never grew into hands with fingers;
envy the things my feet do; tell me
   how to enjoy familiar features.

Winter that blew in like a rumor,
blew in and dragged us out of houses,
turning us into living ghosts who
   wandered around the city grieving,
win back your ruined reputation:
blanket our crimes with tender flurries,
blow back our hair and freshen it with
   patterns of ice beyond believing.

Ivy that sprouted when the cord broke,
sprouted like some old curse and soon had
people inside a haunted mansion
   walking around in savage dazes,
grow as enormous as you want to
but for the sake of comforting, not
trapping the foes who pace the carpets:
   mimic their networks, not their mazes.

Year that looms just around the corner,
looms like another chance at freedom,
study the past and know it cold, but

feel no compulsion to repeat it:
menacing drifts of snow don't last here,
grunts of determined doubt won't work here;
when a new hand or challenge grabs me

may I robustly, fondly meet it.

Chasing Spring

In a certain sense, it was just what he wanted. The green
of her leaves, the healthy roughness of her bark,
the smell of her sap—sweet enough to die for—
meant it was spring. But it also meant she was gone.
Rushing out to meet her altered the weather
but took away a spirit that went with her.

Far below, she chewed on a pomegranate.
The bitter taste reminded her of him,
and how he would growl and sputter when the time
for seeing others came; the half-a-year respite
kept her young cheeks rosy, although sometimes
resentment got in the way of the fun she had.

Making changes in the house too early
caused a minor series of disasters:
the flowerboxes vanished in the frost
and birds, confused by snowflakes in the birdseed,
circled the house with jilted eyes. But when
cold stays, how violent is the urge to say

to the snow, you are frozen as the gate of my soul,
to the hills, you are dead, you are distant and empty, but look!
On the other side of the brook (and here the lies start)
a yellow flower nods in your direction,
in the depths of the lake you thought was hard as granite
a face with a stupid grin is getting bigger.

So much, then, for the habit of chasing spring,
willing the ice to thaw before it wants to.
The eye that sees a bonfire in a tundra
cannot know a false flame from a true one;
the brave, dumb oaf who'd rather swallow poison
than praise its fancy bottle, endures the glacier.

Waiting hurts, and may take more than a season,
but how much better the sudden leaping geyser
than the panting organ, posing as a scorcher;
how revived the mind feels, rounding the bend
to discover there, like a beating heart in the snow,
giving off its own heat, the shock of the crocus.

Duet

The man on the stage, seducing his cello,
does not lift his bow in frustration;
difficult scales do not remind him
of a high window where a woman
waits (same shape, better conversation).
Sound is not a veil past which
he lurks, tongue out, but the topmost spoke
of a wheel whose other spokes include
the sunset, the grape, the bloody motive.

The girl in the pit, corrupting her flute,
raises a few indignant eyebrows,
but they are raised for nothing—it is
the sound and not the shape she longs for
when she leans forward, lips to metal.
Sometimes a flute is just a flute,
and when she leaves the darkened hall,
greeting the night air, she does not seek
a basement, but an adjoining chamber.

Going Public

When your eyes, trained too long on the things that happen
behind dark curtains, scan the marketplace
without the urge to linger, and your body,
told over and over that what means most
takes place in bolted chambers, stiffens up
and saves itself for later, when its thrills
and chills have a built-in finish, so that if
superb odors of saffron, swirls in puddles
dazzle you, you flee (perhaps you'd rather
keep the spice in a box, create the puddle
yourself), when going out is just a thing
you do to guarantee a life of safe
and intimate arrangements, but that life
is running out of substance, and you find
your fondness for the person there is shrinking,

keep talking. Over coffee, over time,
I have as little interest in your mind
as a candle has for the angry hand that snuffs it,
but I'm good at games. We'll play a round of chess
as the regulars watch, and for each piece you take
you'll get another verse of the song they sing
when types like you go home. We'll make a web
of stares, telling ourselves that every time
a thread of vision finds a hook and catches,
another light in the city switches on.

Brief Encounters

i.

By as many times as the framed sets of teeth
have grown, sprouting habits and limbs, you've shrunk—
fine for a past-tense version of what
you do, but somehow, now, giving you
a terrible present. The voice that broke
over cold silence, the face blank enough
to graft an army of faces onto,
seem like romantic cousins of
this urban drudge with armfuls of bags,
and after forced words, you rejoin the crowd,
my coins in your pocket, my stories racing
out of my hands and into your house,
where they break the ice on another couch—
how my life was a finger that others twisted,
how I lamed myself and deserved what I got
but at least made possible the children's
expensive education. Oh stay
totemic and warm in the room where I'm
the only one in your life, the one
who gets up and leaves when the hour is up!

ii.

My elbow, aiming at marble, slipped
and dangled in mid-air. Take a stand?
That was what I could plainly *not* do,
pinned all my ambitions onto,

and like a pro, I wooed my love
with visions of our world: the gap
between a book and those who look
into its spread, unyielding shanks,
the moody, languorous delay
between a parachute's release
and its arrival on the ground,
the mine so full that it caves in
upon its own gold self. My love,
flushed as a fine red wine, replied
"Then never call me yours. That gap
you live to wallow in is filled
by hate, by effort, and by love.
If I make a face and pour
wine in your lap, I planned it that way;
see with what force the tall door slams."

Learning from the Movies

In the world of the high jump, if something can go wrong
it will. First he makes it over but brings
the pole with him; next he jumps too early, landing
up to his neck, upside down, in dirt; finally
he finds the right pace, looks good, gets ready,
and the pole—standing for friends?—falls down.
So he skips off and tries another sport, just as

the sailor who, finding himself in a hall
of mirrors, having seen his lover's husband
shot down, his false lover downed also, struts out
vowing to forget them both. Where we'd stay
and look for wounds on ourselves or our simulacra,
he smells blood and gets out as fast as he can,
as fast as the woman in the big-shouldered suit

who can laugh at a slap and teach men to whistle
settles into the rhythms of an occupied backwater town,
its bar songs and shoot-outs. Not to give up but
to become a wise fool trying; not to linger in
chambers of vain reflection; never to forget that to sing
"Am I blue?" is to conquer blueness—these things
the seeming goners, towers of raw strength, show us.

Holy Days

Whether they spent their time scanning old views
or planning new ones, their voices were more calm now.
But something about their old behavior,
when they discussed it, flustered and confused them;
it was nothing next to their new surroundings
and the ample, gentle people who lived there
except for the times when the odd thing happened.
More and more they were feeling like figures
in a painting who find themselves outside the frame
and, looking in, don't like what they see,
and, creeping backward, attack what they do:
why am I laughing like that? I'd never
hold a glass that way unless I wanted
to prove I was well-off. That was when
another picture started blocking their view:
they were back among the hills where they'd spent
so much time figuring out what it meant
to climb a hill. Every evening
they took in the sky with sweeping, tragic gestures,
a little crazy, but smart enough to know
they were being stupid. Stupidity was the point:
how else could they cope with the lights
that glittered in the valley of every hill
than by ranting and stomping, flapping their arms all the way?

ii.

Yet it was as far from complaining as the paths
where they did their walking were barren or caked with mud.
Thinking fast, talking faster, they made
a different metaphor each time: it's a flash,
it's a carcrash, it's a cloud
around a corner, they'd say, while pills going by
scowled "Them again," or christened them "The weepers."
If these mockers had only known they were
more grist for the hill-top put-downs! The walking dead
for whom night meant a trap could be laid
and hills were things to climb on the way to the market
only fueled the conspiracy
of the bloodshot eyes, of the messy perfectionists,
and when they came back to the hushed apartments,
although the feeling was not one of satisfaction,
it was harder than rocks and, somehow, warm to the touch.

iii.

When hills stay put but climbers go away,
thrills do not end. Tonight, it was
the smell of pine, someone's fancy skirt
whose pale arabesques almost looked like
the plumes of air they'd exhaled in high places
long ago. Outside, the snow went wild,
but inside—that strange effect again
where you're half in, half out of a beautiful picture—
it was clear enough what they both were thinking.
One had picnicked on a mountain and hadn't come down yet;
the other had trudged up hill after hill—
the snowy, the grassy, combinations thereof—   *53*

in love with variety more than with picnics.
It was hard to deny that the state of things
was better, lately: watching snow through windows
lets you insult it. But past skirts, pines, hearths,
something was wrong; their nonchalance rang false;
a minute before rejoining the crowd
they bowed their heads and suddenly saw
the cold hill where their former selves sat
unloved, but loving the view.

Spigot Variations

i.

Returning home from a secret meeting,
needing a drink to face that face,
he saw the blood in the sink and thought

he'd done it now: had she given up hope
and done herself in? This is the life,
the moll in the hotel thought; they even

tint your showers for you. "Dark tea
again?" the spoiled child said, requesting
a weaker brew. They never knew

that running water is subject to rust,
that even the fastest-moving stream is
rosy with the color of where it came from.

ii.

But what about all the timid hoses
that spurt russet water that hits the grass,
sinks in, and weds itself to earth,

a jet of red no longer? It would be
so much better to run the reel backwards
so the wild hose seemed to suck up the soil

and send it down a tunnel the color
of arson, of shame, or better yet
to harness the hose to a pump so strong

it left a deep, indelible stain
on every pale thing under the sun,
on spires and silos, on cradles, on graves.

iii.

The public fountain, pride of the unstable
town, attracted pigeons and people
to its bright side. They loved its flashy,

over-the-top exuberance:
its curls, its swirls. But somehow they knew
never to dip their hands or wings

into its central, sparkling pool:
however loudly the fountain gushed
it kept on coming back to itself,

golden, complete and perfectly
sufficient. Soon the people left,
saving their coins for somewhere else.

iv.

That flood of notes at the end of a life
acts as a dam for all life's floods;
we found him in a pool of his own

blood, his battered head at rest
at last, and next to it, the score—
carefully sealed—of four last songs.

They told the story of a year,
a cycle utterly unlike
a life where surges came and went,

where plugs were scarce, and waves of pain
rushed out in messy, racing red.
Music was what cleaned up the mess.

v.

After the slight I braved the street:
nothing but lean, malicious flames
posing as people, wounded trees

shaking fat fists, a swollen face
watching me with its big red eye.
I believed a limitless tube

traveled from my veins to the stars,
turning there to scatter my blood
on sidewalks. Home again, I poured

dozens of clear cups, thanked my stars
the moment was past. I paced. I thought,
give me that crimson rain again.

Forest Murmurs

i.

People always picture a forest
when the stories of their lives rush too
painfully forward—to forked roads, to dead ends.
They covet its promise: old selves crumble
as much as they love its motto: anything goes;
they put their heads on their desks and dream of dreaming.
It's true that the smallest forest harbors
tolerant bowers, lakes for forgetting.
But woods are not places without patterns
so much as places for patterns other than
ones so familiar they either turn into
• skin-colored grids or bars on the windows.
Only find the right forest, and day residues,
night choices, go spinning among the treetops
like streamers hung for a party long over
but still flooding the scene, the very air
with intricate crossings, gaps that are more than chasms.

ii.

The forest is full of guides tonight.
Hidden in the armpit of one of the tallest trees,
I think I have spotted two main types:
there are the ones who walk around putting
clocks in the branches and tape on the ground,
who carve up bark into jigsaw puzzles
and claim that once you have the knowledge

and the skill to fly over the forest
it takes the shape of a man. And then there are
the ones who go around feeling everything—
from velvety moss to toughest stubble
they've tried it all, but they sometimes forget
protruding roots for the sake of seeing
a muddle where a mystery should be.
Between these groups no looks are exchanged,
a fact which makes me haughtily wonder
why they can't see themselves as I have seen them,
bumping into each other and making
colorful zigzags on the forest floor?

iii.

It was like realizing that the backs
you followed down alleys made you happy
because they all looked like
the back of the boy
who turned to you one long-ago, honeyed summer.
Of course, I realized, perched on a stone.
Of course this is why I keep coming back
to the forest: for all the trunks that stick up,
there are all those magical spaces
between the trees that quietly let you in.

iv.

For four days now I have haunted the places
where low-hanging branches got in my way the most.
Somebody told me that letting twigs lash
your avid, upturned face was a lot

like finishing school—harmless, but not
for the useful or strong. This voice went on
that bringing your mood swings into the wood
splintered the brightest canopy
into dull, grimy, dime-a-dozen leaves.
And for three whole days I wandered and worried,
hearing a voice translate my deeds
into damning phrases: "It's a duel
between secrets and answers, and the answers
are cheating"; "Keep dragging the trees
down to your level, and they'll sprout fingers";
"Any way you cut it, it's graft";
"You're drawn to the forest as saps to saplings,
as lost souls to graves."

                    But the branches
lured me, the branches mangled and made me
into the only traveler
I could ever be. And to be told
in the sweetest, politest possible way
that I'm all thumbs, I'm naive, I'm history
makes me want to shake them up, saying
your cypress is made of corrugated cardboard;
you think your innocent eye sees right
to the heart of things, but what you see
are the firmly shut lids and clammy skin
of your looming corpse. I'd rather be
a baffled, passionate slave to the time
when the bough begins its violent descent.
It's a slap in the face I'd travel forever to get.

Thoughts While Walking

I hate the travel logs that tell you
more about the pain than the place,
yet here I am again, narrating

the same old story to myself
time after time. The papers circling
in an alley, watched by a hunchback,

mimic my plans and their preventer;
when an old man treats the drycleaner
to a lengthy sermon on spotting,

I collect it; bloated clouds spell
messages that people stopped hearing
long ago, and as for the hag

who runs at me, arms open, mouth bleeding?
She's my future, my terrible double.
Always I head out, hot for details,

and always the details start revolving
around brave ingenues who put their
innocent hands in wicked bonfires.

I could never go for ten minutes
without seeing fissures as faces,
and I confess a hopeless weakness

for the types who come back from travels,
gather their fans around and tell them
stories of order or of wonder:

seashores and meadows sometimes get so
muffled and many-voiced that tourists
storm in and do their talking for them—

It's addictive, magical, vital.
But I've observed how, more and more, these
promising outings are becoming

meta-walks and mechanized phrases:
"When I ventured into the outback,
how it blared back echoes of me,

my bright dreams and tragic uniqueness."
Meanwhile forces of good and evil
squirm and flourish under the carpet,

mocking the visionary moment's
sweeping appeal. I'll go on going
out for scenes of horror and pleasure,

but I'll start pursuing clues leading
to the return of that enormous,
fertile ground between shouting and silence.

III

The Triumph of Marsyas

I stood, all pus and muscle, at the stake.
And thinking that was that, you went and picked
your pipes up, snickered, and proclaimed a week
of merriment. Meanwhile a small dog licked

my blood up, causing retching in the crowd.
It was about as much as I could stand
and if, before they flayed me, they had flayed
another man alive, and I had penned

an anthem in his honor, his poor grave
would quake as he rolled over: I'd use trills
to make it snappy, foreign quotes to give
it class, and gongs to complement the bells,

then blithely, crudely pass around a cup.
I did not know what sorrow really meant.
I needed something bad to shake me up.
Torturer, muse, you gave me that event.

Each strip of skin you tore, as if with tongs
(talentless, perhaps, but I was clean!)
renewed my mission, fortified my songs;
I felt the weight, the mystery of pain

and went to my death mortified and stirred.
The men and women in the martyrs' wood

could sense it instantly: I had endured.
So I became their hero and their guide,

and every night I lead them in a dirge
that narrates how we got here; first a shy,
lone voice, then many voices, soar and merge.
Sometimes a fit of sobbing shakes the sky.

Apollo, it was obvious I'd lost
the contest I suggested long ago,
with such grotesque results; but with the trust
and help of thousands, I no longer know;

if you ignore the fact that I am dead
and cannot sing for love, I think I won.
I plumb the darkness while you serenade
your patron, the well-tempered, shallow sun.

A Leper in the City

We all have the same memory
in one form or another. Mine is of
an evening not too long ago when some
volcano or escaping poison turned
the sky and all the city sidewalks green,
making my sickly and inflamed complexion
matter less. Or rather, matter more;
it was as if the people who complain
when I walk by had finally looked hard
and realized that my skin was fit to be
a blueprint for the night. I roamed the streets,
and everywhere I went, somebody had
a funny or a loving use for green—
a woman glided past in chartreuse sneakers,
a baby sucked on limes. Nobody gave
the secret callously away by lifting
me on their shoulders, shouting "Hail the leper!"
That would have gone too far. But I was proud,
and held my head so high I thought I'd touch
the green clouds any second. And of course
the next day, glib, expecting more of the same,
I saw myself reflected in a shopfront
and knew I was the same old, green old eyesore.
Faces got a foot away from me
and crinkled up in horror or relief;
tourists kept their cameras at their sides
until the coast was clear. I was as green
as ever, but the glow of green had gone,
leaving behind a coarse, infected skin

the color of sick leaves, a look that made
a whole town shudder. Vanity is such
an unappealing feature that I tell
the story with a little stab of shame—
better sports than I would say, so what
if you are plagued with raw wounds or mixed feelings?
The city is the same, and you should make
a virtue of repose and meet it on
its own, sane terms. But when you go outside
and due to some alignment in the night
or stirring in yourself, you cannot walk
a block without a sight of green, the thrill
is hard to beat; your beauty is its beauty,
your hue the gossip of the neighborhood.
Was it a hoax? Did I invent it all
deliriously? It was not as if
I stood atop a custom-built, tall building
and ordered crowds to let me call the shots
or else *be* shot; the process was more like
a tender secret that the whole town keeps
with looks that say, we're in on this together.
Tonight, my boils are bad. I never know
when skin will start to slough, and must take care,
when shaking hands, to keep my fingers firm
so that they come back whole. There is a look
of malice and derision in my eyes,
though I am kind. Tonight, a walk is not
the great event it was—for such a night
a leper schemes and dreams—but just a way
of getting from one sickbed to another.
Skulking from mean street to lazaretto
in an ill-fitting cape and in a hurry,
I am my own worst nightmare, I am

too strange to pity, and too green to love.

The Significant Spot

Not long ago I would have breathed a sigh
that put my tiny shadow in its place
by worshipping the world it wandered in.
The view in those days was a real relief.
No sunset told a color to behave
or else be gone; no hill, hellbent on fame,
impersonated mountains; nothing so
familiar as a struggle caused a storm;
instead of armies, clouds both nice and good
clashed in a fruitful manner, bringing rain
that moved me and reproved me where I stood.
No wonder it was pleasant to go out.
But somehow standing there was not enough.
I longed for ecstasies, eccentric deaths
that filled the gap; I saw myself transformed
to dreamy vapor, or impaled on branch,
and came back from my long walks, thumb in mouth.
I never knew that nature struggled too,
that mist rolls down from hilltops not because
it wants to show us what we're missing, but
because it hates the hilltops, and that rain
is not the fertile, jubilant result
of clouds commingling (how the sexy drench
embarrassed me and stirred me where I stood!),
but comes from rapes, and clashes of ideas.
All this was more than big hearts, burgeoning
inside grey suits too small for them, could stand.
They slept more easily if they could set

their growing hopes on a significant,
enduring spot where nothing ever moved
except to gossip, or to say come close
so I can demonstrate the harmony
that death can bring, or memory, or love.
They fled from their apartments, making plans;
they even brought their sisters, if their lungs
were good that day; they hiked, they swam, they climbed;
they looked down at a forest from a hill
and sensed what they had been and might become;
they pined because they were not more like trees;
they stood until they thought they'd sprouted leaves;
they thought the trees were beckoning to them,
but trees have more important things to do.
Some more imagination would have shown
that valleys quake to get the better of
vendettas they inherited at birth,
that when a surface cracked, and strata first
began to form, when rivulets tried hard
to eat the rock away (as crowds appeared
and whispered words like *oneness*), it meant war.

Excerpts from a Botanist's Journal

i.

There is a rose that baffles all the world
but all the world is desperate to see,
if only to be sure of noticing
its crimson head as soon as it appears
among the other roses, arrogant,
unstoppable and sudden as a weed.
It is a flower I could never seem
to find a full account of in my books;
Rose-in-Reverse, I named it in a flash
of inspiration, and the name caught on.
But soon I walked around in clouds of doubt:
what if this freak of nature was a hoax?
What if ambition, eagerness to test
the limits of the field, had made me see
deformities that were not really there?
Yet I could not forget the thing I saw.
While other roses start as timid buds
it bursts up from a garden in full bloom
and then becomes a hard, grey bud again
as petal after petal folds back in;
eyes more attuned to nuances than mine
might see a shrinking flame or a mean fist.
I wrote into the night, describing it;
I heard reports of sightings with a smile
that sent out sympathy and hid relief,
until one morning all the smiling stopped:
the cold had come, the rose was at my door.

ii.

Sometimes I come upon a field in bloom
and think of all the tears I cannot shed;
a swollen dam is bursting somewhere far
below, but as it rises it subsides,
or cloaks itself in cynical disguise.
When I believed aloofness led to love,
was I a fool? How did the drought begin?
I often look at fields imagining
the fields I would have watered with my tears
if I had never bothered with these leaves.

iii.

When I was just a child I liked to watch
a row of flowers turning toward the sun;
I dropped my jaw when ivy grew around
a window, somehow knowing that the glass
could never be a substitute for soil.
I wanted ways to imitate this great
dominion over living things, and if
I couldn't be the window or the sun,
repelling or attracting them at will,
I'd tinker in a greenhouse, I would graft
leaves onto petals, petals onto stems
until I had the kinds of looks I liked.
And now a thousand flowers stand in jars
around my house, all beautiful, all mine,
but their complete obedience has had
an awful cost: I look at them and see
a thousand knees that, hit with the same fist,

respond in unison, a thousand smiles
so stiff they could be bottom halves of masks.
If I still had an empty jar to fill
I'd look hard for a window open wide,
a flower with a passion for the sun.

iv.

I never saw a thing until the day
I found a small blue thistle in the plot
reserved for all my more exotic breeds,
the zinnias and the chrysanthemums
I grew because they were the things I thought
were beautiful before the thistle came.
The sudden contrast shamed me into truth:
the posers never looked so posed as when
they shook their painted faces near the blue,
the thistle stole my heart because, sweet thing,
it could not flaunt its blueness if it tried.

v.

They tell me lilies stand for innocence,
but I could never see it—all those rods
that shoot up in provocative array,
those petals streaked with spots as if they had
a secret or an illness, innocent?
And for this reason I could never pass
a lily without pulling out my shears
and severing the tempter's guilty head.
And while the maimed thing festered in a drawer

I held my shoulders high and proudly wore
a daisy on my lily-white lapel,
I hunted pansies down so I could write
my massive study, *Flowers to Avoid*.
But if I had my job to do again
I'd learn to like the lilies, I would find
a way to keep my scissors at my side
so I could save them for a fairer fight—from
calla to tiger, I would calmly go
and get to know the good ones from the bad;
with one straw basket full of daisies and
another crammed with lilies, I would start
arranging flowers all day and all night,
as if my life depended on that art
and my starved art were gasping for dear life.

vi.

For years I kept a flower by my bed
and counted its grey petals as they fell,
drop by slow drop, away from the red heart;
the more I looked, the faster they came down.
The simple thing had pleased me in its way,
but I could not ignore the power of
sunflowers when they turned their heads from me,
the terror and the freshness of a bud
half in a fallow pasture and half out.
I took the stalk into my own two hands
and threw it in a big can just outside;
I settled back and sang the praises of
an empty vase, and then the flower turned,
because it was no longer mine, to gold.

Tagalong

I'm looking for a war that's big enough
to fill the space dividing you from me.
I know I'm fraudulent, that wishing for
a public version of my paler games
is like excusing filth and slaughter as
the visionary gleam that someone had.
But bleeding privately is bleeding for
no battle but your own; I'm looking for
a war to make my wounds accessible.
When, weary from a showdown with my heart
in which it shook and threatened to explode,
I left my room, I thought I'd see red gore
at every corner. But the things I saw—
the colors and the buoyancies of spring—
pushed the poor thought back in, and all at once
I knew that spatter gets no farther than
my tidy arteries and working veins,
those pumps that keep a vision circular.
How different this becomes when we're at war.
Resistance fighters may insult my cape
and look at me as if I'm worse than dirt,
but I can tolerate their scorn because
I know I'm on their side. The city streets,
smelling of guts and ash, are beautiful
because they set up correspondences
between me and the troops who huddle there:
my secrecy in matters of the heart
recalls the methods of the very brave

who sit around in cellars, plotting ways
to blow the tyrant up; my tendency
to deck my love with lavish attributes—
the power to bring instant peace, make up
for lost time—is a little like the way
a warrior imagines victory;
a simpleton could see the link between
the hole in my life and the flaming gulf
to which my native town has been reduced.
I'm dreaming of a war to end all wars,
although I know I'm sinning when I dream.
Look at the greatest pairs in history
and all the obstacles they had to face—
there's money, family, the tonsure's grip,
seas, towers, traps by rivals, plots by foes . . .
put us beside the frailest of the lot
and see the puny couple we become:
me, fortunate by nature, free by birth
but timid by profession, you aggrieved,
aloof, and anything but adamant,
and ask me then, is it so wrong to see
a villain's smile beyond a picket fence,
a hero by my side, losing a limb?
I'm sane enough to know that war is wrong
but mad enough to go on wanting it,
and here, in a room I'm free to leave, a world
whose borders are dissolving as we speak,
I'm haunted by a vision of a trench
in which a little speck who looks like me
is crouched and cold and frightened. By my side
a comrade writes a war ode, over there
a train arrives on time, and far away,
miles farther than the enemy's supplies,

your face appears, and then your waving hand,

waving—is it a kerchief or a flag?
The vision goes as soon as it has come,
but when I'm fighting in a muddy trench,
careening like a sick goose down a street
I wish were bloodier, or losing sleep
because I have more dreams when I'm awake,
a thrashing war of one, I always see
that guiding, solemn, cautionary hand.

Witness

I crawled out of the wreckage whistling
a bouncy tune, I shut the barbed wire gate
with plots of operas forming in my head.
It was the only way I could go on
without a helpless, horrified look back.
But soon a crowd of mourners blocked my path
and weakened my resolve with their lament:
no song can sound the depths of what you saw,
and even if it could, a song would be
a guilty pleasure after what occurred;
nothing but silence keeps a crime alive.
I walked away with cotton in my mouth
and whispered "No!" when inspiration came;
I told myself that singing would be like
collaborating in calamity.
Time passed. I spoke in grunts and I grew thin,
and then one day I passed a mirror and,
not thinking for a second, thought I saw
one of the walking dead approaching me.
In a great flash of shame I realized that
my thinness was like giving in, and that
my meekness would make men in tall boots smile.
No, it was right to go on signing, and
aggressive, soulful, proud, brash, adamant,
stern, melancholy, loud, not to be stopped,
I filled my lungs with healthy air and gave
my passionate detractors all I had:
they put my broken body in a cage,

but they could never cage my spirit's fugues;
they halted time and bent it out of shape,
but time (not without agony) bent back;
they hated us if we were loud, and so
to quiet down is to admit defeat;
of course it is no easy task to sing,
but singing well might soothe a scar or two;
they burned my family and baked my friends,
but I was lucky, I got out alive;
they thought that, though alive, I posed no threat;
I'll threaten them by proving them dead wrong;
they muffled all the sounds that they could hear,
but never heard the music in my head.

Pomona

It's all about the way you store your fruit,
the things you do to make a harvest last.
I'm often so embarrassingly thrilled
that someone looks my way without a wince
that I spend all my savings in a blink
of someone's lovely eye: plump melons, rich
persimmons and soft peaches fall from me
as if dispersing were the thing that I
was born to do. But these sweet waterfalls
have never had the pay-off I expect—
the faces go, the peaches strew the ground
more suitable for fruit flies than a feast.
And then a risk worth taking comes along
and sizes up my baskets—lighter now,
but still possessing heft—and I release
a stream of fruit, but not the kind he wants:
a hard cranberry hits him on the head,
two shriveled dates insult his open hands.
The starved explorer, puzzled, walking off,
seems like the kind of person who can spot
worms in an apple, beauties in a prune
a mile away. And still he came to me.
What is this lunacy that makes me give
real fruits to wax men, wax ones to real finds?
My system works perversely: seeing mouths
come at me, mad for fruit, I think, you're mad
if you expect you're getting one of mine.

And then a slit eye eyes me with distrust

and I go crazy, raining red again.
I've heard excited rumors of a tree
that keeps a crowd of wanderers well-fed
with plums all summer, lemons in a storm
instead of being, like me, prey to winds
that govern me at all times of the year
except when I expect them. Such a tree
is made of cardboard, if it still exists;
I've been one, and it bored me half to death.
And yet men must be crazy to prefer
my unpredictability to its
delivery of fresh fruit all year long.
All I can say in my defense is that
I'm good for a surprise: discover me
high up on an abandoned, snowy hill
and tell yourself I'm sleepy as the sun
and frail as all the leaves that lie around
and make no protest if you step on them.
Then pinch yourself when you can swear you see
an apple coming toward you, carving lines
in solid crusts of ice; despite the things
you've heard about how winter shuts things down,
the rebel apple blows your mind and makes
the sound of someone skating for dear life.
You check your watch to see what time it is,
you look into my eyes, and still you see
a spot of scarlet in a world of white,
a racetrack where a vain endeavor was.

Surgical Moves

Lights dimmed, the scraper scraped, and I could feel
the change begin; it was the kind of pain
you brace yourself and bear, imagining
all the unfolding options that the cuts
make possible. The red that rolled away
gave rise to thoughts of rolling hills, and so
I told myself, it is a pinch that pays.
Just in the nick of time, I'm hardly doomed
but free to choose my way and free to find
great pleasure in the choosing: jumping off
the table, throwing down the bloody smock
and bolting from the operating room,
I'm the poor fool who stumbles up the aisle
and I'm the sweet face at the other end
who blesses and forgives; I'm in a cloak
behind a pillar, spying on a thief
who answers to my name. Come find me on
the summer lawns, the moonlit winter rinks
and drag me back to where the spongy lumps
coagulate and darken; counsel me
to get down on my knees and look at what
I left behind; implore me to admit
that all the red is realer than the roads
I hastily, unthinkingly pursued;
however many stumps are floating in
the pulp like ghosts of shapes that might have been,
however many stares are telling me to
clean up the mess, it is no mess of mine.

Clubfoot

Meanwhile, meanwhile used to be my limp's
accompaniment. Meanwhile (as my legs
maneuvered an abyss), a ballet is
beginning, and the dancer's perfect feet
propel her downstage, where applause is waiting.
Meanwhile a sad man stomps his gloom away
by stomping evenly: one two, one two
means never blue, his motto goes. But I
was born to other paces, different measures;
the roads I take are undulant and lined
with fluid hedges, trees that take a dive
whenever I am near; a bird's ascent
slows down to an eternal crawl; and when
a doctor's order takes me to the city
it is a jagged gotham, full of spires
that waver in the sky like falling knives
or silver metronomes. Meanwhile, meanwhile
(the rhythm steadied me) a lover steals
upon his mistress with the quietness
that only flatfeet know. So quietly
that he might just as well have stayed at home,
I add when my self-confidence is at
a high point, and the view is at its best.
And sometimes I have thoughts, before the surge
of *meanwhile* drowns them out, that limping is
a thing I'd voluntarily take up
if I were just as upright as the rest:
I see myself, erect, stampeding through

a garden's sturdy, stale geometry
and nearly knocked down by the urge to say
incline, I like your style; ravine, hello;
how many good things share your curvature;
it is the slant of rainfall when the wind
convinces it to drift; it is a sight
that those with level heads and steady feet
miss out on. In a coracle (my new
enthusiasm leads to stories), you
are better, bent; the more you tilt, the more
the water welcomes you, its addled waves
a live reminder of your being there,
its leaping fish a sign that you are still
alert and in command. The clubfoots have
a myth concerning Orpheus' head,
and though I doubt its authenticity
I like the way it goes: hacked off, the head
was rolling down the river, when a change
came over it—it bobbed, it jumped, it shuddered,
it caught itself in weeds, but struggled free
because of all its energy, and then
its eyes began to come to life, as if
a pretty tune enthralled it even then.
Meanwhile his killers marched away, saying
he had his ups and downs. Of course, of course
to hobble is to hinder: sick is sick,
no matter how you change the second term
to suit your needs. But sometimes I am sure
that when I limp along a crooked street,
my dancing shadow is a model for
the stiffs who hurry past without a sound,
showing them *this way*, *this way*, as they reach
the little level huts that they call home.

Magnetism

I stood and let the forces come to me,
and I was never disappointed when
they rocketed around me, one by one.
In that thick field of floating history
there was a richness, an intensity
I never would have felt if I had moved
in younger circles, run with smaller crowds.
The carpets that came straight from long ago,
the wisest words that had been thought and said
became my private satellites, and gave
my daily contact with the outer world
a needed jolt of electricity:
through the exciting orbit I observed
a park bench put a dent in time; a bird
soar in a sky that was not mine alone
but lent its ordinary blueness out
to violent fists that battled for the right
to build a row of houses under it;
dozens of mouths competing for the most
inventive rhyme for *sky*; a giant head
that stroked its chin and mumbled "What is blue?"
and stroked its chin again; a lifeless pair
who, rising up from pages, waved from clouds;
a manic hand that filled a canvas with
famous cerulean immensities.
But when you came, the field got in the way.
It was a thrill to look at you and see
a million details clicking into place,

and it was also scary—when you must
stand for an era, conjure up a world,
you either blunder outright or succeed
unreasonably, dangerously fast:
a single word can make or break a fate,
a certain color clashes with the view.
And when you went away, the field became
a treacherous device for killing time:
the person who returned was different from
the person I had met with in the long,
bright night of absence. And I must admit
the current also made me more afraid;
with all the paths that wound around my head
it was impossible to move without
disturbing all that order, all that grace—
you came to me and, paralyzed with fear,
I held my breath, pretending to be dead.
I can see things a bit more clearly now.
The current was my triumph and my shame,
but lately all the triumph seems unearned
and all the shame is telling me what I
must do to get you back where you belong:
I'll poke a hole in the magnetic field
and open my eyes wide as all the light
I never seemed to see comes flooding in;
I'll reckon up the stares I owe you and,
embarrassed and enlightened, I will spend
another lifetime tendering that debt.

Narcissus on the Move

The time had come to look up from the lake,
and what I saw was promising at first:
a forest to decipher, and a light
beyond the trees, peeped through the morning mist
and made me glad I'd done it. No more days,
I thought, in which the first thing that I see—
my face, downcast or happy—guarantees
whether I loathe or love the lake. No more
insipid, prideful grinning if the wind
decides to send a shapely branch across
my face, or if a passing ray of sun
gilds the dark water, making me dream that night
of incandescent youths and dappled heads.
No more eternal, juvenile delight
in wooing my reflection, eager for
the primal splash, the great, watery oneness.
That was a trap for children and the mad.
The forest seemed to say look up, look up.
And look I did, and look and look, and it
was good at first: to my surprise, the sky
had no affinities with water; it
was big and democratic, while the lake
was tiny and all mine. The flowers which
lined both sides of a path into the woods
had all the thrill of novelty without
the threat, the mystery without the fear,
and when a set of twins came down the path
communicating silently, their eyes

moist discs of mad activity, their hands
gesticulating wildly, I knew I
was in for treats the lake could not provide.
All this took place in seconds. Then I made
the big mistake of asking one of the
amazing siblings what their secret was.
"Don't you realize?" he or she replied.
"We're married, but we're not on speaking terms.
To look in someone else's eyes and see
your own dumb grin come flying back at you—
is our resemblance why we paired off in
the first place, or did sleepy genes kick in
during the years of close proximity?—
can really get you mad. It all began . . ."
But here I ran off, leaving them to stare
their sockets dry; if people could not give
me what I wanted, I would get it from
the world around me. But that world was not
as big or bountiful as I had hoped;
next to the flowers which I had admired
so much I saw, or seemed to see, a sign
that read, "These yellow flowers take their name
from someone who was so in love . . ." It was
enough to make me run again, completing
the story as I went: yellow for cowards.
But running was more difficult this time.
I looked down at my feet and found out why.
Where solid ground had been, all sorts of pools
were springing up: mile-wide pools, shallow pools
and pools that seemed to flow right through the trees,
but what they had in common was the way
they showed the sky: aloof, majestic, with
my baffled, thick head always in the way.

Since there was nowhere left to run, I made

the lake my destination. I took up
my former pose—head pointed at itself
and body stretching toward its twin—and, as
I'd done before, but for good reasons now,
considered leaping in. I'd drown myself
to stop a trend, and when the trawlers came
they'd swear my face was theirs. No, that was no
solution: helping egomania
to flourish couldn't justify a death,
even of such an egomaniac
as me. What I could do, I realized as
I nodded at my face, which nodded back
in dutiful and dull obedience,
was change my way of sitting by the lake.
Instead of staring, starstruck, at myself
I'd keep my head erect, I'd let it swerve
when something pounced or sang, deep in the woods.
Then I'd look down into the lake again
to see how I'd responded. If this gave
my character a certain shiftiness—
the kind that frightens children as they pass—
at least I'd also see the views that are
created when two reels get run at once.
Already I feel changed; I'm listening
to noises in the forest, and my head—
not empty, but not full—is hanging high.
All summer I will pay attention to
the things that turn to gold besides my head
and temper, and in winter I will hail
the snowflakes that invade my hands and hair
with amorous intent, no two alike.

IV

The Lookout

High above the city
my lips are frozen shut, but my mind is saying
come on and turn your head, and the rest will follow.
When I went on about how you let me down,
it was the view and not me talking;
the purple soot that got in my eyes
had me gaping over the railing
at the lights going off and on in the hills,
and when my look returned to my level
could I be blamed if what I saw there
could hardly compare? You were here, you were near,
you were nimble and warm, and you never stood a chance.

Stay where you are, but realize what I went through!
There was so much mist between
the dark streets and the familiar landing
that I never got the views I wanted,
so when you appeared, bright-eyed beside me
and offered to complete the picture,
refusing that offer would have been like
refusing truth or
evading beauty, only I learned that
the beauty was risky—you were the mortar
that was sometimes solid and sometimes water;
your frailty became an excuse
for picking fights—I looked from the city
into your eyes, daring you to live up to it.

Poor beaten-up, toyed-with, well-meaning,
much loved, badly loved, best and
dearest friend, you were the wind
that blew through my fingers; I felt a change coming
and, panicking, decided I saw
taverns and spires reflected in your eyes.
It was a way of controlling weather
and slowing decay. But the city is windy;
seductive, temporary breezes
flood your heart and pull you to it and through it.

There is rain on the railing,
on the rooftops, rain on the highways
and blurring my eyes, rain seeping into the hills
and changing the city lights from hard circles
to soft-edged and short-lived diamonds.
Unless I'm fooling myself, your head is
moving again after all this time.
No more tiny landscapes crowd your eyes,
but that lack makes me all the more eager
to go with you and find out about
the pleasures that the skyline is hiding.
Unless I've ruined my chances forever
here, take my hand and I'll tell you all this
as we go down together, talking all the way.

Rachel Wetzsteon was born in New York City in 1967 and educated at Yale, Johns Hopkins, and Columbia. Her first book of poems, *The Other Stars*, was selected for the 1993 National Poetry Series and published by Penguin in 1994; her poems have appeared in *Best American Poetry 1998*, *The New Republic*, *The New Yorker*, *The Paris Review*, *Southwest Review*, *The Threepenny Review*, *The Yale Review*, and other journals. She has received fellowships from Yaddo, the Ingram Merrill Foundation, and the Bread Loaf, Sewanee, and Wesleyan Writers' Conferences, and currently lives in New York City, where she teaches at Columbia and the Unterberg Poetry Center of the Ninety-Second Street Y.